Time Passes

THE POEMS

of

KATHLEEN DAVEY

All proceeds from this book
will be used to further the work of
The Corrymeela Community

The Corrymeela Press

This book is dedicated to our grandchildren

Andrew, Patrick, Kate,
Charlotte, Raymond, Peter,
Patrick, Caitlin, Christopher

Thanks

To Alan Evans, for his advice, generosity and staying power
To Helen Lewis, for graciously writing a preface
To Alison Curry, for her incisive criticism
To Peter Moss, for his skilful proofreading
and, of course,
To Ray, for his unfailing encouragement and patience

Time Passes
ISBN: 1 873739 09 5
Copyright © 1994 Kathleen Davey
Cover Photograph © Bob McVeigh

Published September 1994 by

The Corrymeela Press

Contents

Preface

Helen Lewis

There is a phrase that we all use from time time: *'Words fail me'* which means that our thoughts and feelings remain locked in ourselves because we lack the ability—or the talent—to express them in words.

Kathleen's words never fail her because they spring from that precious, rare gift of being able to speak through poetry.

Her poems are highly personal, expressing her innermost thoughts and feelings but, in reading them, one feels included in her reflections on life and death, family and nature and the wonders of creation.

There is humour in her poems and sometimes a gentle irony. There is deep compassion for all mankind but also anger and sorrow at man's foolishness and waywardness. Nature in all its manifestations is revealed in astonishing, tender observations.

Above all, there is a shining faith that encompasses all—you, me, the whole world.

Helen Lewis is the author of 'A Time To Speak' — a book of her life and experiences, which included her survival of Auschwitz concentration camp.

Time Passes

I try to catch him up
As he strolls along the shore,
Matching my footprints in his,
His stride no longer
Longer than my own
As in the early days.

Quite clearly he is far
Beyond my reach,
No matter how I try.
I watch the figure—now a tiny speck,
Then stop
And turn the other way.

The prints have gone
Both his and mine,
As if they never were.
The sand is smooth
And flat and clean
Ready for someone new.

November

I love to watch
Starlings in November
Carelessly sliding
On currents of air
And leaning
On the wind
Without flapping.

And see
The small, pale leaves
From my silver birch
Fluttering down
Like hosts
Of cream
Butterflies.

Sunday Worship—Corrymeela

Head bent against the relentless wind
I stumble on towards the Croi
And the sea
In the lee of the Main House.

Rounding the corner of Sean's playground
I lift my eyes and stunned I stop
To watch half a glorious rainbow rise
From the east edge of Rathlin
And pause right over the Croi.

There at the peak
A single seagull hovers motionless
While a sudden shaft of sunlight
Splits the clouds over Knocklayde
Illuminating the 'dove'.

Will this annunciation last
Or must the curtain fall again?

Good Friday—Then And Now
(For Frank Wright 1948-1993)

Head wounded—arms outstretched,
A thief on either side
On whom He set a loving gaze.
Despite a sense of being alone,
Abandoned by His friends,
"He looked for pity, but none was there,
And comforters, but He found none".
By far the deepest hurt of all—
He felt abandoned by His God.

No need to kick against the pricks,
Simply accept what comes.
"Father, forgive them.
For they know not what they do."

Head wounded—arms outstretched,
Hands clasping ours, the one on either side
Frank sat, fixing a loving gaze
On each in turn.
No time for many words,
No trace of pitying self,
Only a radiant peace,
A gratitude,
A sweeping certitude of being

Held and loved by countless friends,
As near to him as if they too sat here.
But far the greatest thing of all—
He felt the unseen presence of his God,
Cradling him, assuring him
That all is well.

No need to kick against the pricks
Simply accept what comes.
'All is forgiven. I'm free to be,
In this life or the next.'

Remembrance Day In The Croi

Howls of wind screech through cracks,
Rain, belching from leaden skies
Pelts like bullets on the plastic dome.
Noise, disturbance, clash of wills.

Inside the curved white walls
Of the little Croi
A silence,
As a score
Or maybe more
Of people drawn from sundry parts
With hearts wounded and bruised
From lifetime buffetings and hurts
Assemble to pray.

The pale, wavering flame
From a lone candle
Gathers together their imploring prayers
And drifts them heavenwards.

The bread and wine are blessed.
Each unto each passes the plate, the cup,
Remembering not only that first time

Our Lord had done the same
And given us the trust to do likewise,
But thinking back in pain
Of those who lost their lives
And those ones left behind
Whose lives will never be the same.

Heaven and earth are full of Your glory.
Backwards in time our minds can see
From earliest days those faithful few
Who—high and low—met to break bread.

The unseen cloud
Of those who have gone before
Surrounds us,
Lifting us from the slough,
Assuring us this is the harbinger
Of the world as it should be,
Where rich and poor, east and west
Clasp the other in embrace
And say: *The peace of Christ to you.*

The whole wide world of earth and heaven
Past, present and future too,
Are linked together in this common act.

Refreshened and renewed
We leave the silence of the Croi,
More able now to face the storm outside.

Daisy Bud

A few days before Christmas
In a crack in the concrete
Blasted by sleet and hail
An ordinary scarlet-stained daisy bud
Quietly announced
Spring is coming.
Peace is coming.

In spite of the blasting
In spite of the frosty words
In spite of the concrete slabs
Peace will come.
For the tear-stained hearts
Of the ordinary people
Announce it.

Snow

The snowstorm is past.
The patch of old cabbage,
The dog stains on the grass,
The weeds on the pathway,
The crack in the fence
Have all disappeared.
Through snow—the great leveller.

On a hospital visit
In search of my friend
I pass people all ages
And classes of life
Roadsweeper and duchess,
All suffer the same
Through disease—the great leveller.

I stroll through the cemetery
Past once lively people
Now dead and decayed.
The agnostic, the Christian,
The Moslem, the Jew
All share the same fate
Through death—the great leveller.

Infant Hope

What good is it to me
If you should say:
*I love you very much
But for you I have no hope?*

Love is wide—
An overarching arm.
Faith is hard to grasp—
A darkly depth.
But hope is:
*A newborn Child
A new idea
A new beginning.*

I love you, Infant Hope.
My faith
I place in you.

Transformation

Uninvited on the door of the garden shed,
Unnoticed had it not been for the sheen
Of sunlight slipping between the leaves,
The web slick with rain made a rainbow
Like shot silk in the shimmering breeze
Or a gossamer stained-glass window.

Uninvited too that insidious fiend,
That silent growing cancer, destructive and cruel,
Unnoticed except for a sense of unease
And a wearisome pain she shared
With her doctor who quietly said:
"I'm afraid you have cancer".

Some time later I visited her in a Home
For victims afflicted likewise.
Her face looked quite radiant as never before
Which posed questions deep in my mind.
Must we wait for ill fortune before we achieve
A deep sense of peace and a heavenly smile?

Roisin

The screeching and squabbles of gulls
On the garage roof
Vying for pieces of fat
Has stopped
Leaving a soundless blank.
The jubilant barking of Max up the road
Announcing that day has begun
Has also stopped.

Less than thirty miles away
Far from the busy town
Two gunmen masking human beings
Burst in upon a loving home,
And brushing past young Roisin Cairns
Who thought their garb was just a prank
On her eleventh birthday,
Barged straight into the telly-room.

Then out into the dark they sped
Concealed by night,
Leaving behind a special gift for her,
Two brothers dead.

Drumnakeel Souterrain
(For Andrew, aged 17)

Scrambling up the steep and shaggy grassbank,
With caution skirting jagged shrubs of gorse,
I reach the top.
There I see a hole—two holes in fact,
The entrance to a cavelike refuge home,
Two thousand years lying hidden in the ground.

All kinds of pictures hover through my mind
Of how our ancestors escaped their foes.
How could they fashion such a place as this,
Gigantic stone precisely placed on stone?
Without our modern tools how could they move
Those massive solid slabs that form the roof?

Imagination takes its hold on me.
I picture how they surely must have felt,
Crouching in fear beneath this sandstone vault,
Alert and listening for an alien sound,
Just like a fox escaping from a hound.

Or did they sometimes feel like in the womb
And when the moment came to squeeze outside
Did it appear to them a kind of birth?
Or was it like a parting from the earth
As all of us must do, as time goes on
When we are born into a sunlight realm.

Sharing

We share our soil, we share our sky,
The trees in the woods,
The streams that flow by,
How is it then
We don't know how
To share each others' lives?

Perhaps we have no soil to share,
And woods and streams seem far away.
The street is where our children play.
Could that be why
We don't know how
To share each others' lives?

Vulnerable

How often does his tortured heart
Show a quality that is unique?
Perhaps he has failed a crucial exam
Or tried vainly to find a new job,
Perhaps unexpectedly out of the blue
He's been told he has cancer.

Maybe his partner has given him up,
Or a child has been tragically killed,
A loved one must now live in a wheelchair,
Or in a world of her own which is worse.
He touches raw edges of anguish and grief
And tastes all the meanings of hell.

If he rises above it and trusts in his God
Who suffers and feels with us all,
He will find a new level of love and peace
And an empathy till now denied
With those who wear masks to cover their scars
From the unflinching gaze of the world.

Minnowburn Re-Visited

Today's a day of magic—
Red and yellow and different shades of bronze,
A trelliswork of boughs against the cloudless sky,
While underfoot the rustle of crisping leaves,
Scattered at the feet of the 'elephants legs'
Of the Minnowburn beeches.

This is the spot where I saw my first kingfisher,
Just by the bridge at the turn of the road.
A dart of rainbow colour skimming the stream,
Away and out of sight.

But that was almost fifty years ago.
We then were newlyweds.
This was our home—a paradise for us,
When we were unencumbered,
Free to roam and live and love.

Springtime was here and we were young,
The War was past and nothing could go wrong.
Time has moved on and we are growing old,
Another 'war' engulfs us
And it will not go away.

Would that Time could halt its flight
So we could drop our anchor
For just one single day.

The Rock

There is a rock in Donegal
That is more than twice my size,
It peers above the gorse shrubs
As if looking out to sea.
It split in two.

So what is strange in that, you say,
To split a rock in two?
So many ways come into mind
How this could be achieved—
By earthquake, storm or avalanche.

But what was strange and startled me,
When looking close at hand,
Was to see at the top a tiny shoot
With a root two foot long
That split the rock.

If a seed alive and growing
Can split this rock in two,
Could not the seeds that we are sowing
Slash hatred's barrier through?

To Margaret

Where did you get that pretty brooch,
That ring of pearls with garnets six?
Surely they clearly represent
Your children joined in warm embrace.

That brooch I treasure to my heart,
It was a gift to mark the day
When over fifty years ago
Our lives were joined—for ever one.

But look—I see a stone has gone
And left a space where it should be.
That brooch will never be the same
Five stones instead of six.

Do not despair—that stone's not lost
But safely waiting in a place
Where one by one more stones will go,
Cherished and guarded from all harm.

And in his own appointed time
The Master Craftsman will restore
Each garnet to its proper place
And make the circle whole once more.

The Daddy-Longlegs

Endlessly he scales
The kitchen windowpane,
Free to move, but not free to be.
The window opens—swiftly he slips out
To freedom, up into the blue.

A swallow ceaselessly circling
In search of a meal,
Swerves and swoops
And snaps him into his beak
So this is freedom.

Which do we choose?
To stay behind the windowpane
Safe without aim
Or risk leaving
Our warm, familiar home

And step outside.
Free to be—
Or to perish.

The Dragonfly
(For Raymond, aged 10)

Struggling to free himself from his cocoon,
Wriggling and squirming, a new-minted dragonfly
Waits to be born.

Up on the riverbank, close to the rushes
An old man, aware of the stress and struggle,
Puts hand in pocket, withdraws his old penknife
And, with gentle care, splits the small creature free.

Feeling the warmth of the air on his body
Slowly he pushes his head through the skin.
On new weakling legs he climbs one of the rushes
To dry his useless unused wings in the sun.

A dart of bright blue skims over the water
In the wink of an eye the dragonfly is gone.
A hungry kingfisher squanders no moment
In finding a morsel to garnish his meal.

> *So this is freedom—*
> *Which do we choose?*
> *Remain unambitious*
> *Or struggle and strive*

To shake off the shackles
That smother the light?

For conflict is good
And though painful the fight,
Our sinews grow strong
And help us to face
All the hurts and the pains
Of our human race.

KATHLEEN DAVEY

The Greenfly

With massive hairy legs
And multifaceted eye of scarlet red
Surveying all around,
He cautiously strides across the slide
Beneath the powerful lens
Of my young son's microscope.

What fearsome beast—
A marvel of creation.
Yet what is so special
About this masterpiece?
Are there not billions more
All just the same?

Yesterday I casually
Squashed a dozen dead.
Does our Creator
Treat His children so?

The Hedgehog

Why do you always answer me
With such a spiky tone?
Or else you curl up in a ball
Glum, sullen and alone.

I think I understand a bit
Of what you really feel.
Your inner side, your tender side
Is hurt and will not heal.

Sometimes I've seen you open up
And share with us your soul,
Then comes along some intruder
And back in your ball you roll.

Hedgehog-like aren't most of us
Usually playing a part?
Only with a chosen few
Can we trustingly bare our heart.

Autumn Leaves

Caught up in an autumn beech storm
A wild gust of wind swirls the leaves
Like brown scraps of paper they scatter
All over my face and hair.

It brings to my mind distant days
Trundling aimlessly homewards from school
Unhurried through mountains of leaves,
Welly boots going *swish, swish* all the way.

Today I avoid crunching leaves
And sedately step out of their path
Forgetting that long ago thrill
Of those autumny sounds and smells.

Perhaps we all feel this dull ache
Of parting with something we've loved
But the eyes and ears of the innocent child,
Have somehow been lost on the way.

April Raspberry Canes

If I should try
To paint that early growth,
I'd need to find a new-born green
That I have surely seen
Elsewhere.

Perhaps it's like
The penetrating green
You sometimes find
On mossy stones
Among the cones
In a damp pine-wood.

Or even more it's like
The startling green of wispy sea-weed
Found in a pool
That's full
Of furtive creatures
That hide from view.

Like all things new
It will in time grow old.
That new-born green
Like us,
Will lose its charm,
Curl up and fade away.

Two Gifts

Two precious gifts I've inherited
Over many a passing year.
The first one my mother bestowed on me,
The second my father dear.

Her gift was a deep sense of gratitude
For all and for everything.
Each day, be it sunny or wild or wet
Through the house you could hear her sing.

Bless the Lord, O my Soul, and do not forget
To rejoice and give praise every day.
Who forgives you and heals you, feeds and protects you
Be sure to give thanks—she would say.

At times we would laugh at her unfailing thanks,
Like the day when she dropped on the tiles
A trayful of glasses and two of them broke.
It might have been four, she smiles.

The gift from my father was relevant too
In the world as we know it today.
Wherever you go, or whatever you do
Never lose a sense of wonder, he'd say.

I remember quite vividly one summer's eve
While in Scotland on holiday
From a late game of golf we were taking our leave
When our eyes turned the other way.

There stretched out a sunset of crimson gold,
Hectic red streaked with ribbons of greys.
The heavens declare the glory of God
He whispered low and continued to gaze.

On a clear autumn night he'd look up to the sky
And ponder long thoughts on creation,
How galaxies formed and life beyond space
He would contemplate long with elation.

At times in the garden, attending his flowers
He would bend down to pick up a creature,
And study it creeping right over his hand,
Amazed at each delicate feature.

I treasure these gifts, for true gifts they are,
But gifts are for giving away.
In joy I bestow them on our children now
And in turn to their children one day.

Leaving School

I have reached the Lower Sixth of time,
Only one more stage to go
Before I leave "school"
And enter a new wide world.
Some of my friends are in the class above
And will be leaving soon.
Others have left before they reached the final stage.
I miss them still.

These years have been good years
And almost cloudless.
Time has not lagged.
Days too short, always engrossed,
Learning to live and love,
To sing and dance, paint and play,
To wonder at the world around
And beyond.

I love these years of school
And do not wish to leave.
There is so much to do and get to know.
But how I miss those friends already left.
Even so we still can keep in touch,
Although we cannot linger face to face.
What love and trust we shared in earthly days
Will be transformed and stronger
In that world to be.

Eastermeet

Very early in the morning
Though no longer dark
I strode briskly up the hill
To meet the Day—
That day awaited
For six long Lenten weeks,
The Day of Easter.

Already life was vibrant in the fields—
The alto bleat of sheep
Tuned to the treble voice of lambs
Frolicking at their side,
One lamb indolently
Lay curled upon its mother's back.
Hedge sparrows joined in all this exultation,
A robin sang a grateful solo song,
Accompanied by the steady, silver trickle
Of a hidden spring.

Gazing across at the stillness of Rathlin,
Lying sleeping on smooth sheets of water,
Undisturbed, I stood alone,
Yet not alone, for in that morning hour
I felt a Presence near me,
Assuring me that it was real, that Easter long ago,
That it is real—the Easter of today.

The black, the pain, the death
Have been transcended
And life's meaning is made plain.

So when that dreaded day
Of grief and separation
Arrives to crush us,
We need have no fear,
For Easter is at hand
And we are not alone.

Time
(For Patrick D)

The things I will mend
When I have some more time—
That fruit bowl to stick for example,
Wedding present to us nearly fifty years back
And broken for twenty-five of them.

Those mauve and grey gloves,
Painstakingly knit
In an intricate Fairisle for Mother—
No, for Granny, for that's what she usually was,
And indeed what I am, I admit.

That reliable clock that simply won't go,
Can't have *very* much wrong,
I'm convinced.
The battery's good, I have checked up on that.
I can't think just what else I could do.

When it comes to the bit
And the family has gone
And the days and the hours are much longer,
These trifles that pass simply mean less and less,
Love of friends and of hobbies grows stronger.

Caravan Holiday

This is a day for a fire
Of winter logs,
An Aran sweater, fleece-lined boots,
An armchair and a gripping book,
A favourite record faintly in the rear.

What shall we do
With our bright coloured deck-chairs,
Our swim-suits and sun-creams,
Those smart shorts and sandals,
Racquets and golf clubs?

It seems we should wait
Till some time around Christmas
For our mid-summer holidays.
And simply curl up in a rug and pullover
For our caravan break in July.

Stalemate

The poppies are bowed
Reflecting how we mortals feel,
Waiting for warmth
To rouse our sap
And make us look up and be glad.
No stirring, no movement,
Glum stillness, all feelings suppressed
Is there no hope?

I look up to the sky
For a pale hint of blue.
None is there.
I watch two carefree swifts
Playing magical 'tig'.
Perhaps away up there
They can sense the sun's warmth.
They chide us to shake off the gloom.
One day this stalemate will end.

Wet Day

Sweet peas have stopped stretching to the sun,
Ferns, forgetting to unfurl,
Stand motionless,
Drizzle drips from the trees,
Dampened daisies, drooping in the grass
Shut their eyes tight.

Slugs slowly slouch among the undergrowth
And gorge on growing strawberries,
While snails, protected by a house of shell,
Aspire to higher planes
And nibbling neatly as they trudge
They scale the raspberry canes.

Large oriental poppies, petals peeling off,
Hang helpless, stagnant, still.
In spite of all this gloom
Strings of diamonds
Glisten
On the washing line.

Vitality

Is it right to enjoy to the full
The joys and beauty of life,
The sweet smells of roses and thyme,
Savour raspberry, orange and plum,
Stroke the fur coat of your cat
Or bumble your hands in the stream?

Possibly not
I decide,
Letting the soft rain
Of July
Slide gently across my
Upturned face.

Growing Old
(For Peter, aged 5½)

I love the noise
Of girls and boys
With all their toys
And make-believe,
Their dressing up
In high-heeled shoes
And painting noses
As they choose
In different shades of red.

I also love the solitude
Of strolling through a shady wood,
And if I could
I'd make a tape
Of all that serenading song,
The blackbird whistling to his mate
Quite unaware
That I am there.

How will it be when I am old
And stiff about the knees
And feel the cold?
No longer crawling on the floor
A growling bear behind a chair
Ready to pounce.

No longer strolling through the wood,
Unless some kindly grandchild should
Agree to push me there
In my wheelchair.

How happier far to be like this
With mind alert
Than body fit and trim
And mind inert.

Homeless
(For Kate, aged 9¾)

Sitting comfortably
Quietly enjoying her evening meal,
Without any warning
She suddenly felt
Her whole house
Cave in.

Sharp shards pierced her skin.
Shocked and bemused,
At first
She dared not open her eyes.
Soon one
And then the other
Surveyed the scene.

The horror, the total destruction
Shattered her.
The only sound she could make
Was a low huffle
That nobody heard.
There she was
Still living but homeless.

That poor benighted snail
Caught in my wheely-bin.

Spider's Web

I went to open up
The greenhouse vent
To let in autumn air,
And was amazed to find
A spider's web,
Suspended from the roof.

It shimmered in the morning sun
And I stood still
To watch the spinner
Purposeful and swift
Scamper around the ring,
Fulfilling fast the task it had begun.

Entranced, I watched this living speck
Weaving the finest gossamer,
As if instructed from within.
At last, the web complete,
It scuttled to the centre
For a well earned rest.

I then remembered what my purpose was,
To open up the vent.
Lifting the latch I pushed,
Wiping out the tenuous strand

That held it to the roof,
And in the twinkling of an eye
The web was gone.

How often in these awful times
Do casual careless acts reach out
And rip our very lives apart.

On The Park Bench
(For Caitlin, aged 8½)

She quietly settled, leaning on my arm,
Quite unaware I might not want it so.
Laden, a heavy bag on either side,
She gave a little tremble and a shake,
Her fur coat gleaming in the glowing sun.

No doubt exhausted from her long day's work,
She looked for rest before her journey home.
Just when I thought that she had gone to sleep,
I looked at her, but there what did I see?
A whirr of wings! Goodbye my Bumble-Bee!

To The Bombers

Does it matter losing your dad,
When you're little more than a lad?
You don't have to show that you're sad,
When they brag about all that their fathers
Are able to do.

Does it matter losing your mum?
It's the end of the world for some.
The day will eventually come
When the pain and the parting some day
Will overtake you.

Does it matter losing your child?
You remember the first time he smiled
In his cot—now he's killed.
An innocent victim of only
One year over two.

Father, mother and child—all are gone,
Leaving hearts strangulated and torn.
Could it possibly be there is born
A seedling of love and forgiveness
That makes all things new?

Flotsam

Rudely awakened
I lose my dream
Which melts and drifts away,
While I vainly struggle
To grasp the vaporous trails,
At last concluding
That there's nothing there.

Why do I squander
So much of my energy,
Wielding the muck-rake
For flotsam and jetsam,
So much unimportant,
Mere wisps of reality,
While there above me,
Should I but straighten
And look,
Is the coveted treasure
That all of us seek.

The Two Friends

Tall, slender,
Slim and graceful,
Draped in a delicate robe
Of shimmering green,
She gently sways,
And on tiptoe
Peeps through our bedroom window.

But see her now,
Stripped of her dress of green.
She wears in its place
A cloak of fine lace,
The pattern intricate
And flecked with silver gems.

Beside her stands her friend,
Stocky and stout,
Their arms in loose embrace.
She dare not lean too close
For he has such a prickly face.
These two stand sentinel
Both night and day,
In summer's heat and winter's chill.
Long after we have left this earth

They'll keep their vigil still,
My silver birch,
My rugged hawthorn tree.

The Sunflower

Tall and lofty
You look down on me.
Warm and golden
You reflect the sun,
Your multifarious eye
Surveying the earth below
Where soon you will begin
A hundred other lives.

How many days
Before you droop your head
And you will be no more?
And you, the sun,
Are you so mortal too?
How many days
As at the start of time
For you to go?

Paradox
(For Frank Wright 1948-1993)

That glowing rose,
Exuding life and hope
Will wither soon
And be a twisted twig.

That dry gnarled stump,
As dry as any bone,
Surprises us,
When warmth of spring
Draws out a hint of green.

What of our dearest friend
A wraith, an empty shell?
That brilliant brain
That all embracing smile
Snuffed out?

The paradox again.
What seems to us as dead,
Emanicipated now
Bondless can roam
And enter hearts and minds
Unfettered, as in the days of clay,
Fulfilling now the task he'd just begun.

So let us live this life we know
Right to the hilt with thanks and joy,
Remembering that it merely is
A shadow image of the life to be.

Old Age

Will you tell me the truth.
Do you really feel old
Propped up in your chair
With your hair newly rolled,
Your face small and wrinkled
Your hands gnarled and lean
Do you really feel old
Or quite different within?

Is it more like the feeling
Of wearing a dress
That you've worn far too long
And it just feels a mess?
But inside that garment
So threadbare and small
Is the genuine you
Hardly altered at all?

You sit half the day,
They think you're asleep.
Inside you're alert
And ready to leap
Into days of the past
When the family was young
And you reigned supreme
Both by hand and by tongue.

It's strange growing old
And we notice it not,
Till our eyes lose their sight
And our teeth start to rot,
Our hearing grows partial,
Life draws to an end.
By the time all this happens
Death comes as a friend.

KATHLEEN DAVEY

Hospital Visit

From the fresh and frosty air outside,
I enter in where it says 'Push'
And am met with a smell—
A mixture of ageing and cabbage.

I pass down through a series of wards
Those who used to rule the roost
Supreme in their own homes,
Now at different stages of that downward trend.

In the first ward, they notice you.
One smiles or nods or says a word.
One holds a book—another knits.
In the next ward one only sits.

In Ward Three here you see
Fine faces look vague,
Active limbs dwindled to matchsticks
Or else swathed in bandages on oozing ulcers.

Now I approach Ward Four.
My friend for nearly forty years lives here.
Her neighbours sunk in chairs sit in a circle,
Not listening to television which never stops.

It even drowns the moan and cry:
"*Nurse, nurse... I want my mammy.*"
It even drowns the carefree song
Of the budgerigar—also in a cage.

Despite all the love the nurses show,
Their deep devotion and their word of cheer,
Preserve me, Lord,
From such a growing old.

"Le Mouvement—C'est La Vie"

I found a blackbird yesterday,
Crashed on a window pane.
Lifting it gently in my hands
I felt it shake and shudder
As if in pain.
Warm it was, but fearful,
Its yellow beady eye
Observing me
"An enemy or friend?"

Some moments passed.
I held it fast
Then with a little flutter
It drooped and died.
Its eyes were closed,
All movement ceased
It became stiff and cold.

You people in high places who
Wear politicians' guise
Must surely see that movement
And ever open eyes
And the power to bend and flex
Are things we can't ignore
If we seek for that aliveness
And peace on earth once more.

Gordon
(In memory of G.A.E.B. 1915-1990)

Last night you came to visit me,
So I could say 'Goodbye'.
A year ago we knew full well
That time was short and yet somehow
We could not say the words,
But let the time tick tiredly by.

We talked of days of long ago,
Those far off days of youth,
Of Norman with the "silver spoon",
Of Dulwich, Campbell boarding, both
Of which you missed,
But without rancour.

With love and deep affection too
You spoke of Sheila tenderly.
"Amazing girl—such stamina,
No doubt passed on
From Amy's Scottish grit."

It was Edwin that you dwelt on most,
And questioned pensively.
"What was it happened in his youth
That changed him right around,

For happen something did?"
And so it was the time was up
Homewards I had to fly,
We never said the parting word,
That final word *"Goodbye".*
Strange you should come astride a horse,
Our tartan on his mane.
Strange too that it was at 'The Manse'
That we should meet again.

You stooped to let me kiss your brow,
I raised my hands to touch your face,
A shudder and you were no more,
Then I awoke with nothing left
But an uncertainty.
"Which is the real," I ask myself,
"The waking or the dream?"

Mirror Image

See him, the toddler,
Pattering towards me
Arms fully outstretched
>   To be embraced now,
>   Across my breast.

Look at him later.
"Oh, not the milk-jug!"
"Don't touch that hot poker!"
>   Everything is novel,
>   It must be tried.

Who have we this time,
Struggling and kicking,
Screaming and fighting
>   Against all those grown ups,
>   Against *"those who know better"*.

Look at that young face
Asleep in his cot
Clutching his teddy
>   Ready to waken
>   To greet a new day.

See him the young man
Now drawing close to her
Arms fully outstretched
    Just to embrace her
    Against his chest.

Look at him later
Trying the impossible
Bikes, mountains, drugs,
    Everything's novel
    It must be tried.

Who's that we see now
Fighting for liberty
Shouting and screaming
    Against wrongs that degrade
    Against *"those that know better"*.

Look at that old face
Asleep in his coffin
Clutching his faith
    Ready to waken
    To greet a new day.

Horn Head
(For Patrick C, aged 11)

Swallows swooping low
And swerving,
Sure prophets of the weather.
Baby butterflies, speedwell colour,
Flitting on golden buttercups.
Ants, anticipating where we'd sit,
Attacking the underside.

Breezes, drenched with the honey-scent
Of myriads of pink clovers.
Industrious bees, honey-bags full,
Droning like bagpipes.
Seagulls, screeching relentlessly.
Incessant flies
Fearless of flicking.

Today at Horn Head.

The Glory And The Grey

The sweep of mellow pink arching the sky,
Mingles with translucent opal shades
Behind black sleeping hills.

Two tawny hares appear,
Hopping haphazardly over Lottie's field.
Crows, wagtails, starlings, gulls,
Chatting, squawking, reeling, swooping,
Exuberant with life.

A silence falls and in awe,
We are waiting expectant.
All is still, soundless.
All seem aware that
Something is about to happen.

Then out of pale amber behind Downings hills
Appears a flaming rim,
Almost imagined at first,
Then deeper
Until it becomes real and red and round.

As it rises and grows,
The glory fades from the sky.
The magic is broken, the stillness has gone.

Gulls dabble again in the shallows
Grubbing about their business.

I turn around
And retrace my steps in the sand,
Following the tracks of countless birds,
Small and great,
Tracks of their previous elation.

What does it mean
This Glory then the Grey?
My eye fixes on a blood-red lifebelt,
Hanging on a wooden cross on the sandhills.
Could this be the answer?

The Glory has been displayed
For all its awe and beauty—
The ordinary has been transfigured.
The vision now has faded:
We are left with a stark cross
Against the reredos
Of a grey granite mountain.

That cross of suffering is all around us,
Year by year
Red like the lifebelt on the shore.
Yet it *is* a lifebelt,
His suffering for us was not in vain,
It was the birth pang of Easter.

The Sapling

Out strolling down the winding path
That passes through the forest
I came across a seedling spruce
Pushing its way through unrelenting tarmac.

"What chance have you," I thought,
"Of growing into a tree of beauty and of use?
I leave you there and you will die,
Half-grown, unnoticed, valueless."

So bending down I prised it out,
Drew it from its barren bed,
And in Corrymeela let it sink its roots
And mix with other trees.

How many of our young people,
Conditioned, captured, caged,
Must think in strictly party lines,
Throats throttled if they venture out of line.

Lift them from that hard tarmac
Of bigotry and hate,
In new surroundings stretch their roots,
Expose their minds, give them a proper chance.

So through the years in spite of fears
Another generation will be born
To save our land.

The World Must Be Crazy

A tycoon in New York
Paying a fine for drug-pushing
Of six million dollars
Still has twelve million left.

A few miles away
In a derelict suburb,
A child sells her body
For the price of a meal.

They bury a small boy
In far Guatemala
In an old cardboard box
And on it is printed:

General Electric
Progress our best product.

Another Incident

"The forty-four year old man
Shot in the head
In front of his wife
This evening
Has died.
He was named as..."

The remaining report
Falls on deaf ears.
There's a meal to prepare
The time's getting late
And we've heard it before
Ten times in eight days—
Just another incident.

We don't see the scene
Of the husband and wife
Approaching the gate
Of the place where they work
At a job they accepted last week.

We can't see the Sierra
Stop close to the pavement,
A youth in dark glasses

Spring out of the car,
Place a gun at the man's neck
Fire three rapid shots
Speed away down the road
Out of sight.

We don't see the man fall,
Blood gushing,
Wife screaming
Or two children, aghast,
Stop their play.
Or the young passer-by
In direct line of fire
Freeze,
Thinking he too will be shot.

*"Do I run or lie down
Or comfort the woman?"*
No time to consider
He instinctively bolts,
Zig-zagging to safety,
Madly pounding the locked doors
To alert the security
And gasp out the news.

We don't see the five children
Bereft of a father,

Facing the bleak days ahead.
We've heard it before.
But time's getting late.
I must cook the potatoes now
And stir up the soup.

Goradze

The hospital is shattered,
Twenty-eight killed.
Perhaps they are the lucky ones,
For what the anguish of those left to live,
Half-living, mutilated, blind.

The youth who fired the fatal shell
Can't see the wreckage he has wrought.
(He simply obeys orders, nothing more.)
No more can we—too busy with *our* war
To contemplate Goradze in its plight.

We die here drip by drip,
Just one by one and tit for tat.
But should these drips
Be gathered into one—
What carnage.
Three thousand souls
Who should be living still,
Swept out of sight.

The human mind's not built
To take it in.
A single loved one lost
Is all the world it seems.

Circles

I like to think of life in circles,
The earth itself, the sun,
The pathway of the planets, of the moon,
The horizon seen from a mountain-top.

The Celtic "caim" drawn through the air
Depicting God, the encompasser
The Chinese 'yuan', 'united' and 'round',
Their Autumn Family Festival.

What have we done to our circles on earth?
To the circle of family life?
Or the families built into communities?
Or the nations' round table talks?

You can't draw a circle just out of the blue
Without a fixed central point.
Until we can find it right at the heart,
We can never complete the arc.

But once we have found it, our eyes can turn in
To the centre, our arms stretch out wide
To those on each side of us, offering support,
While receiving from them in return.

My Cactus

Despicable, prickly
Cold-hearted globule
Jagged and hurtful
Tearing the flesh.
How is it possible
Out of such desert
For six soft golden flowers
To unfold in the sun?

If you were a person
I'd always avoid you
For fear of being pierced
By the stab of your tongue
But maybe inside you
Just like my sharp cactus
Are those warm-hearted flowers
To unfurl in the sun.

My lovely, hateful cactus
What is your name?
I shall call you
Schindler.

Hidden Roots

I contemplate my birch-tree over there,
Trunk, branches, twiglets bearing leaves,
And underneath the soil, buried from view,
The taproot, side-roots, countless rootlet webs,
A mirror image of the tree above.

It makes me think how similar we are,
The helpless ones dependent on the strong,
The strong of no avail without the weak
And both together gradually would die
Unless they drew upon the hidden sap
That nurtures and sustains all life.

The Following Light

There is a line in a well-known hymn,
Sung frequently today,
I puzzle that it says: '*O light
That followest all my way*'
Surely it should be reversed,
I following the light.
What is the good of just darkness ahead
When you're groping alone in the night?

I pondered quite long on this baffling thought
Lying wakeful in bed one night.
*"If the light were to shine on each step that I take
What's the need of our faith"* I thought.

It very rarely happens
That we see the way ahead,
But looking back on past events
We find we have been led.

It only is in retrospect
We see the way was planned,
And even when we've made mistakes
There was a guiding hand
That brought us back on to the path
That was the best for us.

Mystery

The more I'm acquainted with various faiths
The less sure am I they are wrong,
While the deeper I delve and experience my own
The more certain I am it is right.

Who dares to package the Creator and say,
"Life's simple enough to explain"?
Life is sheer mystery—a paradox,
A collage of joy and pain.

To look up at the sky on a clear starlit night
You are blinded by wonder and awe,
As also to gaze on a red velvet rose
That has neither blemish nor flaw.

So beauty and might are a part of our God,
But what use is the loveliest rose
When bursting with joy you want to give thanks,
Or the stars when your hold on life goes?

Perhaps it sounds childish or naively vague
To say you can talk with God,
Creator, sustainer of all that has breath—
Yet once on our earth He has trod.

All life is a mystery, our brains are too small
To contemplate all of the plan,
But the mind that designed it once wore human flesh
And exposed God's true nature to man.

At the heart of the universe there lives a God
Showing love to the death for our sakes,
Saying death's not the end but a newness of life
Beyond all that we now comprehend.

Not far far away in some heavenly home
But more close than we're able to see
He's our constant companion
Through rough and through smooth.

That's surely sufficient for me.

Silver Jubilee Song
(Corrymeela 1965-1990)

O God, our help in ages past,
Our praise we bring to You.
Years back in us You put your trust
A special task to do.

In questing hearts and doubting minds
A tiny seed was sown.
You watered, nurtured, guarded it
And see how this has grown.

That fragile group of seeking folk,
Now scattered far and wide,
Responded blindly when You spoke
And trusted You as guide.

Though five and twenty years have sped
Since first we heard You call,
We know that Your wise hand has led
And helped us through it all.

Three thousand lives shot dead and maimed
Are easy words to frame
But what the hurt, the grief, the pain
When you know one by name.

O God, our help in ages past,
Our praise we bring to You.
Still be our Guide while 'Troubles' last
And make our country new.

The Sea Holly

Outside my window grows a shrub,
No special shape or sheen or hue,
So inconspicuous that you
Might call it dull.

No ceonothus startling blue
Or lilac mauve or fuchsia red,
Just dull and boring as I said,
With no surprise.

But look again! My shrub has changed.
The Spirit of the wind has blown
And quite another side has shown
We never knew.

Each branch displays an energy,
Each leaf a greyish silver shade.
My shrub has come alive and made
Me think aloud.

What of our Church—to most so dull,
So unrelated, so outworn,
What if the wind of the Spirit were born,
Transforming all?

LimboLand
(For Charlotte, aged 12)

Have you ever visited LimboLand
Halfway between wake and asleep?
Or sometimes it goes the other way round,
Halfway between sleep and awake.

For me it's my favourite part of the day,
Or the night it could equally be,
When my body's asleep and my mind floats away
Over mountain and desert and sea.

In bed I curl up in a positive roll,
Still aware of some audible sounds,
And widely I travel all over the world
In impossible leaps and bounds.

I visit them all in Edinburgh,
In London and also in Wells,
And nearer to home unseen I may join
In all of their whoops and yells.

So if you fall asleep immediately
Or waken up on demand,
You'll never know the sweet ecstasy
Of sleep-wake LimboLand.

Three Years Old
(For Christopher, aged 4½)

You said this was God's house
But God is not here,
I can't see Him anywhere
Do you think He's near?

He's not in the pulpit
He's not in the choir
Perhaps He is hiding
Right up in the spire?

Mummy was silent
Not knowing what to say
To her three-year old son
At church his first day.

Next week in the park
It was stormy and wild
And mummy went walking
With her questioning child.

Oh, look at the wind, Mummy,
Look at it playing
Chasing the dry leaves,
The bare branches swaying.

"I can't see the wind, son,
Neither can you,
We can see how it's powerful
And the things it can do.

Perhaps that's how God comes
For each one to see,
Not just a great Person,
But in you and me."

Anxiety

How much of our energy
Is wantonly wasted,
As we play morbid games
With yet unborn time.

Losing the present,
Unsure of the future
Which may never contain
The dread that we fear.

The help for that future
Will not come today.
When tomorrow's today,
He's affirmed—*I'll be there.*

First Day At School

I well remember
My first day at school,
Wearing black button-boots
With thirteen shiny buttons,
Clutching my slipper bag
And long metal button hook,
Age six, I set off.

I look at my grandchild,
Her first day at school.
Totally unconcerned,
Harlequin anorak,
Mickey Mouse lunch-box,
Self-fastening trainers,
Age four, she sets off.

What of her grandchild?
How will she dress for school?
More likely than not
She'll not go there at all,
With some silicon-based unit
Linked to her monitor,
Age two, she'll switch on.

Suffering

The problem of suffering
Troubles me deeply.
There are some who believe
It was intended to be
That one should bear pain
To bring about goodness.
If you take away suffering
No need would there be
For humility, sympathy
A greatness of heart.

One hundred times no,
This cannot be.
What loving Creator,
What kind of a Monster
Could carefully calculate
How much destruction
He should pour on His people
So as to achieve
Humility, sympathy
A greatness of heart?

Devise concentration camps
Gas chambers, tortures,
Watch small children die

Of disease and starvation,
Inconsolable mothers
Looking helplessly on.
Could instigate earthquakes,
Ignite volcanoes, discharge tornadoes
To trample mankind
Just in order to create
Humility, sympathy,
A greatness of heart?

Suffering lies right
At the heart of the universe,
Each of us meets it one day.
But God has revealed
Through Jesus, His son,
That He suffers too through it all.
He gives no guarantee
To protect us from pain,
His promise is only to share it.

Clones

We want a baby
The child of our dreams
Strong, handsome, healthy,
Intelligent, bright,
Artistic, musical
Preferably male.
We'll go to the Clones Bank
And see what's for sale.

We press the blue channel,
(Pink for a girl)
And study the holograms
Of those who've been 'born'.
This might do
Quite like you
He's tall and dark
Aged twenty-two.

Some in stock?
What good luck
Going half-price
Past 'Sell-by' date.
Out with the credit card
Two satisfied customers,

Modern genetics
Create a new world.

Pray some calamity
Wipes out humanity
Before we take over
As God.

The Familiar Face

When we come to slip our moorings
And meet our Maker face to face
That face will have a look
We've seen before.
We may see our ageing friend
Whom we visit every week,
Or the hunched up child
Who lives in a wheelchair.
And the countless other people
Whom we've known and loved on earth
Will welcome us
As many times before.

Should this surprise us?
For has He not said—
As you do it to one
Of the least of my friends,
You are really doing it
To me.

The Corrymeela Community

The Corrymeela Community is a group of Christians in Ireland, both Protestant and Catholic, who believe themselves to be called together as "an instrument of God's peace" in the Church and in the world.

The formal members of the Community (of whom there are about 170) work in close co-operation with **The Friends of Corrymeela** (of whom there are about 1,200 in Ireland and throughout the world) and others who share their commitment to the work of reconciliation.

Corrymeela runs a centre at Ballycastle with accommodation for up to 120 people. It is used as base where people from different traditions meet and talk freely and also serves as a refuge for victims of violence. Conference and education programmes concerning the roots of social conflict are developed through staff workers in the areas of Youth, Church, Schools and Community Work. Every year over 8,000 people in some 250 groups visit the centre.

Corrymeela House in Belfast is an administrative office, a base for field workers, a meeting place for Corrymeela groups in the city and a resource for many groups who share some of the aims of the Corrymeela Community.

IF YOU WOULD LIKE TO KNOW MORE ABOUT THE WORK OF CORRYMEELA OR WOULD LIKE TO BECOME **A FRIEND OF CORRYMEELA** PLEASE CONTACT:

THE CORRYMEELA COMMUNITY
CORRYMEELA HOUSE
8 UPPER CRESCENT
BELFAST BT7 1NT
TELEPHONE (0232) 325008